THE LITTLE BOOK OF
CAMPING

Camping Is Easy . . . If You Know What To Do!

D1476506

Written by Zack Bush and Laurie Friedman

Illustrated by Sarah Van Evera

THIS BOOK BELONGS TO CAMPER:

_____

DEDICATED TO YOU, OUR WONDERFUL READER

Have fun camping!

CAMPING
is easy. And fun!

You just have to know what to do.
Ready to learn?

First, pick a place.
Woods are nice.

But a backyard or
a bedroom works too.

Or create
your own.

Now it's time to pitch a tent.

It doesn't have to be fancy.

You'll need a sleeping bag.

PICK THE SLEEPING BAG YOU LIKE BEST.

Don't have one?
Don't worry.

A blanket works just fine.

Add a pillow.

PICK A PILLOW
TO GO WITH YOUR SLEEPING BAG

A flashlight.

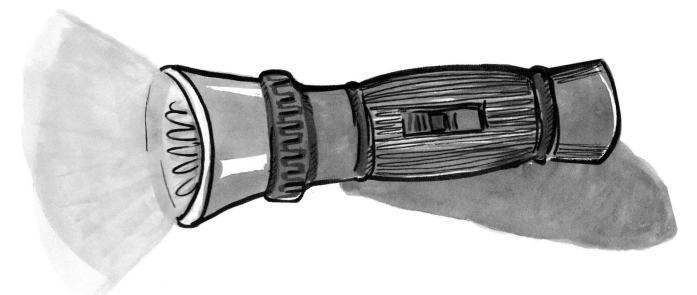

And a friend.

Or two.

Better yet, a whole bunch
of them!

CAMPING

is even more
fun with snacks.

Especially marshmallows.

To get them toasty brown,
you'll need a campfire.
Or an oven.
And a grown-up!

REMEMBER . . . SAFETY FIRST!

Never make a campfire without a grown-up.

Guitars go nicely with marshmallows.

So do harmonicas.

And singing voices.

When it gets dark,
shine your
flashlight and
see what
shapes you
can make.

There are so many fun things you can do when you go **CAMPING** with your family and friends.

STORY TELLING

STAR GAZING

GAME PLAYING

Having fun
together is what
it's all about.

QUESTION:

When is it time to go to sleep in your tent?

ANSWER:

When the moon is high and the sky is filled with twinkling stars.

See! **CAMPING** is easy
once you know how
to do it.

CONGRATULATIONS!

YOU'VE EARNED YOUR CAMPING BADGE.

Now you're ready to pitch tents,
roast marshmallows, and shine your flashlight.
Have fun **CAMPING!**

Go to the website www.thelittlebookof.com
to print out your camping badge.

Keep reading all of the books to
learn new things and earn more badges!
#thelittlebookof

Made in the USA
Columbia, SC
29 July 2020